Pierre Gasly

The Boy Who Loved Cars - Turning A Passion Into A Profession (A Motorsport Biography For Kids)

Trisha N. Logan

All rights reserved. No part of this publication may be reproduced, distributed, or transmitted in any form or by any means, including photocopying, recording, or other electronic or mechanical method, without the prior written permission of the publisher, except in the case of brief quotations embodied in critical reviews and certain other noncommercial uses permitted by the copyright law.

Copyright © **Trisha N. Logan**, 2024.

Table Of Contents

INTRODUCTION

1. VROOM, VROOM! MEET LITTLE PIERRE
Zoom Zoom! A Childhood Filled with Cars
A Family Of Racing Enthusiasts
The Spark that Ignited a Lifelong Passion

2. FROM TOY CARS TO GO-KARTS
The Thrill Of The First Race
Learning To Master The Go-Kart
Early Victories And Growing Confidence

3. CHASING CHECKERED FLAGS
Stepping Up The Competition
Facing New Challenges And Rivals
The Fuel That Powers Pierre's Racing Dreams

4. FORMULA DREAMS TAKE FLIGHT
The Big Leagues: Entering Formula 4
The Winning Formula
Pierre's Star Begins To Shine

5. THE ROLLERCOASTER RIDE
The Highs of Winning : Zoom Zoom To The Top!
Facing Setbacks and Disappointments
Turning Mistakes Into Turbo Boosts!

6. THE FRENCH FLYER
Zooming For The Tricolore!

France's Racing Hero
Inspiring Young Racers: Pierre's Pit Crew Of Dreams

7. NEVER GIVE UP
Pierre's "Never Give Up" Spirit
The Secret Ingredient: Hard Work And Dedication
Turning Dreams into Reality: From Toy Cars to the Real Deal!

8. LIFE IN THE FAST LANE
The Fast And The Furious... Off The Track!
The Glamour And Excitement Of Race Day
Balancing Act: Racing, Friends, And... Laundry?!

9. INSPIRING THE NEXT GENERATION
Follow Your Passion And Chase Your Dreams
Believe In Yourself And Never Give Up!
Hard Work: Pedal To The Metal!

CONCLUSION

GLOSSARY
Zoom Zoom! Your Go-To Guide To Racing Lingo

FUN FACTS ABOUT PIERRE

Trivia

INTRODUCTION

Imagine a world where every thought, every game, and every dream revolves around fast cars, shiny cars, and cars that go **ZOOM**! That was the world of Pierre Gasly, a boy who didn't just like cars; he was absolutely **crazy** about them! From toy cars scattered across his room to posters of sleek race cars on his walls, Pierre lived and breathed all things racing. He even drew racetracks on his homework when no one was looking!

Pierre Gasly: The Boy Who Loved Cars is the thrilling, heart-pounding story of how one car-obsessed kid turned his wildest dream into reality: racing in the biggest, fastest, and most exciting car races in the world Formula 1! Get ready to travel with Pierre from his playful days of zooming toy cars across the floor to the electrifying moment when he raced his very first real-life go-kart, his heart thumping like a racing engine. You'll cheer for him as he speeds past rivals and faces the toughest challenges on the road to becoming a champion.

Pierre's journey is a lot like the high-speed turns of a Grand Prix race filled with ups and downs, surprises, and moments of pure adrenaline. From his first go-kart race, where he felt the rush of speed for the first time, to his climb through the ranks of junior racing leagues, Pierre's story will take you on a ride full of excitement and perseverance. He didn't win every race, but every loss fueled his determination to be better, faster, and stronger. And that's what makes Pierre's story so inspiring.

But this adventure isn't just about racing around tracks at breakneck speeds (though that's pretty awesome too!). Pierre's story is really about chasing your dreams, no matter how big or impossible they might seem. It's about working hard, staying focused, and never giving up, even when the road ahead looks rough. Sometimes life throws unexpected twists and turns your way just like a tricky racetrack but Pierre shows us that with enough passion and courage, you can navigate through anything.

More than just a racing tale, this is a story about believing in yourself. Pierre's journey teaches us that no matter where you start or how many obstacles you face, you can achieve your dreams if you stay driven (pun intended!). Whether you're dreaming of racing, painting, inventing, or anything else, Pierre's story proves that with a lot of heart and a little bravery, nothing is out of reach.

So, whether you're a die-hard fan of all things racing or simply love a good underdog story, **Pierre Gasly: The Boy Who Loved Cars** is a must-read. It's the perfect mix of excitement, adventure, and inspiration for a book that will spark your imagination, ignite your dreams, and show you that with enough determination and passion, the sky (or the racetrack) is the limit!

Are You Ready to Rev Your Engines?

So, what are you waiting for? Buckle up and get ready to join Pierre on his incredible journey. Feel the rush of the race, hear the roar of the engines, and experience the joy of chasing down your biggest dreams. With fast cars, fierce competition, and a whole lot of heart, this story is a reminder that **anything** is possible if you're willing to go the distance.

Start your engines, and let's hit the road to adventure!

1.

VROOM, VROOM! MEET LITTLE PIERRE

Zoom Zoom! A Childhood Filled with Cars

Have you ever felt an overwhelming, all-consuming love for something? Maybe it's dinosaurs, painting, or exploring the mysteries of outer space. For a young boy named Pierre Gasly, born on February 7, 1996, his passion was all about cars. And not just any cars we're talking about super-fast, zooming race cars!

From the very start, when little Pierre was just a toddler crawling around, he was enchanted by anything with wheels. Imagine his parents finding him pushing toy cars around their house, making playful engine noises, and building race tracks out of blocks and pillows. His eyes would light up with joy every time a real car zoomed by on the street. He'd wave enthusiastically, daydreaming about the day he'd be behind the wheel of a real race car.

Pierre's family shared his love for cars, especially his dad, who was a racing enthusiast himself. They often spent time together watching races on TV, cheering for their favourite drivers and talking about every exciting moment. As Pierre grew from a curious 5-year-old into an eager 8-year-old, he soaked up all the details about different cars, racing tracks, and strategies to win. It was like discovering a thrilling new world filled with speed, excitement, and endless opportunities.

Special occasions like birthdays and holidays were extra exciting for Pierre because they meant getting new car-themed toys! His collection was impressive: tiny Formula 1 cars, remote-controlled racers, and even a pedal-powered go-kart that he raced around the backyard. His room was like a mini car museum, with posters of famous drivers and model cars neatly arranged on shelves.

Pierre's fascination with cars went beyond just playing with toys. Even as a young child, he was curious about how they worked. He spent hours taking apart his toy cars and trying to put them back together, fascinated by their engines and gears. He would bombard his dad with questions about car mechanics and engineering, always eager to learn more.

As Pierre grew older, his passion for racing grew stronger. He started devouring books about racing, watching documentaries on famous drivers, and attending local karting events. By the time he was 10, he was determined to become a race car driver. This wasn't just a passing childhood fantasy; it was a powerful dream that drove him forward.

Pierre's childhood was filled with the joy and thrill of cars. It was a time of exploration, discovery, and dreaming big. Little did he know, his journey was just beginning, and it would lead him to places he had never imagined, all fueled by the same passion that ignited his dreams as a child.

A Family Of Racing Enthusiasts

In the Gasly household, racing was more than just a hobby , it was a family tradition! Pierre's family shared his enthusiasm for fast cars and thrilling races. His dad, in particular, was a huge motorsports fan who even tried amateur racing himself. He would share exciting stories of his own racing experiences with Pierre, sparking the boy's imagination and desire to follow in his footsteps.

Weekends often meant heading to the racetrack as a family, buzzing with excitement. Pierre's eyes would widen as he watched the colourful cars speed by, the roar of the engines vibrating through him. He would study the drivers closely, marvelling at their concentration and skill, cheering loudly for his favourites, and feeling his heart race with every lap.

But it wasn't just about watching races. Pierre's family actively supported his interest in racing. They bought him books and magazines about motorsports, took him to car shows, and let him play racing video games.

They saw the spark in his eyes and wanted to nurture it, helping him chase his dreams.

Family gatherings often turned into lively discussions about the latest races and drivers. Pierre's grandparents, aunts, uncles, and cousins would join in, sharing their opinions and predictions. It was a wonderful bonding experience, bringing the family closer together through their shared love of racing.

Pierre's family wasn't just supportive; they were his biggest cheerleaders. They believed in his talent, drive, and potential. Their encouragement gave him the confidence to pursue his dreams, push his limits, and never give up, no matter how tough things got. They were his foundation, his source of strength, and a constant reminder that with passion, determination, and family support, anything is possible.

The Spark that Ignited a Lifelong Passion

Picture this: a little boy, not even five years old, sitting in the passenger seat of his dad's car. The windows are down, the wind is blowing through his hair, and the sun is shining brightly. As his dad revs the engine, the car lurches forward with a thrilling rumble. The little boy's eyes widen with excitement, his heart races, and a huge smile spreads across his face. He feels the rush of speed, the power of the car, and the joy of the open road.

That little boy was Pierre Gasly, and that moment was the spark that ignited his lifelong passion for cars and racing. From that day on, Pierre was hooked. He couldn't get enough of the sensation of being in a car, the thrill of speed, and the adventure it brought.

Every car ride became an opportunity for Pierre to dive deeper into his new passion. He would ask his dad endless questions about how the car worked, study the dashboard's dials and gauges, and even pretend to be a race car driver, making engine noises and shifting imaginary gears.

Pierre's love for cars went beyond the excitement of driving. He admired the design and elegance of the machines. He spent hours looking at car magazines, drawing pictures of his favourite cars, and marvelling at their sleek lines and powerful engines.

But it was the world of racing that truly captured Pierre's imagination. He would watch races on TV, cheering for his favourite drivers and feeling the excitement as they zoomed around the track. The skill, strategy, and determination of racing captivated him.

Pierre's passion for cars and racing wasn't just a fleeting interest. It was a deep love that would shape his future and drive him to achieve remarkable things. That spark, lit on that sunny day in his dad's car, would grow into a powerful flame, propelling him to the top of the racing world. It was the start of an incredible journey, one that would take him from a car-crazy kid to a Formula 1 superstar.

2.

FROM TOY CARS TO GO-KARTS

The Thrill Of The First Race

Imagine a young boy named Pierre Gasly, just nine years old, standing at the starting line of his very first go-kart race. His heart feels like it's drumming a wild beat, his hands are all sweaty, and his tummy is doing flips like he's on a rollercoaster. He's a mix of nervous, excited, and a tiny bit scared, but most importantly, he's all set for this big moment.

Pierre has been dreaming about this day for as long as he can remember. He's spent countless hours zooming around his backyard in his little pedal-powered go-kart, pretending he's racing against the world's best drivers. He's studied every curve of the track in his imagination, practised turning smoothly, and tuned his skills to perfection. Now, it's time to see if all his practice has paid off.

When the flag drops and the race begins, Pierre's heart races with excitement. He presses the gas pedal, and his go-kart rockets forward like a shooting star. The wind rushes past him, making everything blur, and the roar of the engine fills his ears. It's an explosion of sensations, but Pierre feels right at home. He's focused, determined, and completely in control.

He zips through the other karts, guided by his instincts. He takes each turn with care, gripping the steering wheel tightly. Every moment is thrilling; he's not just racing—he's soaring through the track.

When the checkered flag waves, signalling the end of the race, Pierre crosses the finish line with his heart still pounding and a big smile on his face. Even though he might not have come in first, he's experienced something magical. That race was an incredible adventure that will stay with him forever.

That first race wasn't just a fun day for Pierre; it was a turning point. It solidified his passion for racing, ignited his competitive spirit, and set him on a path toward greatness. It was the beginning of an amazing journey, leading him from local go-kart tracks to the grand arenas of Formula 1. It all started with that first exhilarating race, where he tasted the thrill of competition and knew, deep down, that he was meant to be a racer.

Learning To Master The Go-Kart

Imagine you're Pierre, a kid who's just discovered the super exciting world of go-kart racing! You've had your first taste of zooming around the track, and now, you're totally hooked. But just like learning to ride a bike or play an instrument, becoming a great racer takes lots of practice, patience, and a whole lot of fun!

At first, things weren't all smooth sailing. Pierre had to learn all about racing, and there were a lot of new things to figure out! He had to learn how to control his go-kart, make turns without spinning out, and pass other drivers without bumping into them (oops!). It was like learning a new language, but instead of words, it was all about speed, timing, and control.

Luckily, Pierre had some awesome teachers to help him: his dad, who knew a lot about racing, and some friendly go-kart instructors. They taught him the basics, like how to use the gas and brake pedals, steer smoothly, and read the track. They also gave him important safety tips because, while racing is a blast, staying safe is super important too!

Pierre practised over and over again, zooming around the track. Sometimes he got frustrated when he made mistakes, but he never gave up. He knew that the more he practised, the better he'd get. And he was right! Little by little, he started to "master the wheel." He became more confident, his turns got smoother, and he began passing other drivers with ease. It was like he and his go-kart were becoming one, working together perfectly.

But it wasn't just about practice; it was also about having fun! Pierre loved the feeling of the wind in his hair, the excitement of the race, and the friendships he made with other racers. Racing wasn't just a sport for Pierre; it was a way to connect with others who shared his passion.

As Pierre kept learning and growing, he started to win races. It wasn't always easy, and sometimes there were close calls and nail-biting moments. But with each win, his confidence grew, and his dream of becoming a professional racer felt more real.

Pierre's journey from a beginner to a skilled racer is truly inspiring. It shows us that with dedication, perseverance, and a lot of fun, we can achieve anything we set our minds to. So, the next time you're learning something new, remember Pierre's story and keep practising! You might be amazed at what you can accomplish.

Early Victories And Growing Confidence

Imagine the thrill of crossing the finish line first, with the checkered flag waving and the crowd cheering your name! That's the kind of feeling Pierre began to experience more and more as he got better at go-kart racing. It wasn't just about winning; it was about the journey, the hard work, and the growing belief in himself with each victory.

At first, those wins were small, like beating a friend in a friendly race or winning a local competition. But each win was like a little boost, making Pierre believe in himself even more. It was like collecting puzzle pieces, each one bringing him closer to his big racing dreams.

Remember the feeling when you finally ride a bike without training wheels or ace a spelling test you studied for? That's the kind of confidence Pierre was building with every race he won. He was proving to himself that he had what it took to be a champion.

But it wasn't just about trophies and medals. With each win, Pierre learned valuable lessons too. He learned how to stay calm under pressure, make quick decisions, and push himself to the limit without giving up. He was becoming not just a faster driver but a smarter and more resilient one as well.

Perhaps the most important thing Pierre gained from his early victories was the unshakable belief in himself. He started to see that his dreams were within reach. He knew that with hard work, dedication, and a bit of luck, he could achieve anything.

Of course, there were still challenges. Some races didn't go as planned, and there were times Pierre felt discouraged. But he never let those setbacks stop him. Instead, he used them as fuel to work harder, learn from his mistakes, and come back stronger.

Pierre's early victories were more than just wins on a track. They were stepping stones to becoming a champion, showing the power of passion, perseverance, and self-belief. They proved that even the biggest dreams can come true if you're willing to put in the effort. So, next time you face a challenge, remember Pierre's story and keep pushing forward. You might surprise yourself with what you can achieve!

3.

CHASING CHECKERED FLAGS

Stepping Up The Competition

Imagine you're playing your favourite video game, and you've just conquered all the easy levels. You're feeling great, right? Then, you unlock a new, much tougher level with challenging obstacles and tricky surprises. This is what happened to Pierre when he moved from go-karting to junior formula racing. It was like moving up to the most exciting, challenging level in the coolest racing game!

All of a sudden, Pierre wasn't just racing with kids from his local track. Now, he was up against the best young drivers from all over the globe! These competitors were serious about racing, and they all had one goal: to win. The cars were faster, the tracks were longer and more complex, and the competition was fierce. It was like going from playing in your backyard to competing in a massive stadium packed with enthusiastic fans!

Pierre realised he needed to raise his game if he wanted to keep winning. He had to train harder, learn faster, and be braver than ever on the track. No longer just a kid who liked cars, he was now a serious competitor with a big dream.

Think of it like this: imagine you've just unlocked an amazing new car in your racing game. It's super fast, but it's also harder to control. You need to master how to handle its power, make sharp turns without losing control, and use its speed to win the race. That's exactly what Pierre had to do with his new formula racing car. It was faster and more powerful than anything he had ever driven, and it required a lot of skill to master!

But Pierre was up for the challenge. He took on the tougher competition, the faster cars, and the more complicated tracks with enthusiasm. He knew that every race was a chance to learn, grow, and show that he belonged in the thrilling world of high-speed racing. He was ready to prove himself.

So, next time you face a challenge that seems a bit intimidating, remember Pierre's story. Stepping up to a new level can be exciting and a little nerve-wracking, but it's also a fantastic opportunity to learn and discover just how amazing you can be!

Facing New Challenges And Rivals

Remember that video game level we talked about? Well, it's about to get even tougher! In junior formula racing, Pierre wasn't just up against harder tracks and faster cars; he was also competing with some incredibly talented rivals. These weren't just kids who liked to race; they were determined, skilled, and eager to win.

Think of it like this: you're on a soccer field, but now you're playing against top teams from across the country. Each team has its own star players and secret tactics. That's the kind of competition Pierre faced. Every race felt like a mini-championship, with everyone pushing themselves to the limit to be the first to cross the finish line.

Some of Pierre's competitors were older, more experienced, and had been racing for years. They knew the tracks inside out and had a lot of tricks up their sleeves. They were fast, fearless, and ready to push the boundaries to get ahead.

It was a completely new experience for Pierre. He had to quickly adapt, study his opponents, and predict their moves. It was like playing a high-speed game of chess where every choice mattered and each move could change the outcome of the race.

There were moments when Pierre felt like a small fish in a big pond, but he didn't let that stop him. Instead, he used it as motivation to work even harder and push himself further. He knew he had the talent and drive to compete with the best, and he wasn't going to let anything stand in his way.

One of the most exciting aspects of racing is its unpredictability. Anything can happen on the track, which made each race thrilling for Pierre. There were close calls where he narrowly avoided crashes, daring overtakes, and moments of pure joy when he crossed the finish line first. There were also disappointments when things didn't go as planned, but he used these experiences to learn and improve.

Through it all, Pierre never lost sight of his dream. He saw every race, every challenge, and every rival as an opportunity to grow and become a better driver. He embraced the competition, the pressure, and the excitement of racing. Each race brought him closer to his ultimate goal: becoming a Formula 1 champion.

The Fuel That Powers Pierre's Racing Dreams

Have you ever wanted something so much that you were willing to do whatever it takes to achieve it? Maybe it's learning a new skill, like playing the guitar or mastering a skateboard trick. Or maybe it's a big dream, like becoming an astronaut or a famous artist. For Pierre Gasly, that burning passion was becoming a Formula 1 racing champion. And nothing was going to stop him!

Racing at such a high level isn't just about having talent; it's also about working hard, staying dedicated, and never giving up, even when things get tough. Pierre understood this and was ready to put in the effort. He was like a superhero, driven by his love for racing and his unshakeable determination to succeed.

Imagine training for a marathon. You can't just wake up one day and run 26 miles! It requires months of preparation, early morning runs, and pushing your body to its limits. Pierre approached his racing career in the same way. To be the best, he had to train like the best.

His days were filled with practice, both on and off the track. He'd spend hours at the gym, building strength and stamina. He worked with coaches to improve his driving skills, analysed race data to understand his performance, and even practised on simulators to get familiar with different tracks.

It wasn't always easy. There were early mornings, late nights, and missed gatherings with friends. Sometimes, Pierre felt exhausted or disheartened, but he never let those feelings get in the way of his dreams. Every drop of sweat, every extra lap, and every sacrifice brought him closer to his goal.

Pierre's dedication wasn't just physical; it was mental too. Racing is a high-pressure sport where split-second decisions are crucial. Pierre learned to stay calm under pressure, stay focused on the task at hand, and ignore distractions. He was like a laser beam, focusing intently on his target and never losing sight of his goal.

But perhaps the most important part of Pierre's success was his unwavering determination. He never gave up, even when faced with setbacks or disappointments. He learned from his mistakes, picked himself up, and kept pushing forward. He was like a race car engine, always revving up and ready to go the extra mile.

Pierre's story is a powerful reminder that with hard work, dedication, and a never-give-up attitude, you can achieve anything you set your mind to. So, the next time you're working towards a goal, remember Pierre's example. Keep pushing, keep striving, and never lose sight of your dreams. Because with enough determination, you can turn those dreams into reality!

4.

FORMULA DREAMS TAKE FLIGHT

The Big Leagues: Entering Formula 4

Imagine you're an amazing video game player who has mastered every level, even the super-difficult ones. Then, you get invited to join a professional gaming team! That's how Pierre felt when he got his big break to race in Formula 4. It was like moving from the minor leagues to the grand stage of professional racing!

Formula 4 is like a crucial stepping stone on the way to Formula 1, the most prestigious racing series in the world. It's where young drivers get to show they have what it takes to compete at the top. The cars go faster, the tracks are trickier, and the competition is tougher. It's like going from playing in your backyard to performing on a huge global stage!

Pierre was overjoyed about this chance, but he knew it was going to be tough. He'd be racing against the best young drivers from around the world, and the pressure would be intense. But Pierre was ready. He had been dreaming of this moment for his whole life, and he was determined to make the most of it.

Think of it like this: you've been practising soccer for years, and now you've been invited to try out for a professional team. You're excited but also a little nervous to show what you can do. That's exactly how Pierre felt when he climbed into his Formula 4 car for the first time. It was a dream come true, and he was ready to give it his all.

The first few races were a whirlwind of new experiences. The cars were incredibly fast, the tracks were unfamiliar, and the competition was fierce. Pierre had to learn quickly, adapt to new challenges, and push himself harder than ever before.

There were moments of doubt, of course times when he wondered if he was good enough for this level. But Pierre didn't let those doubts defeat him. He reminded himself of all the hard work he'd put in, the sacrifices he'd made, and the people who believed in him.

And then, it started to happen. Pierre began to find his rhythm. He understood the car better, learned the tracks, and figured out his rivals' strategies. He started winning races, moving up the rankings, and making a name for himself in Formula 4.

It was an exciting time for Pierre, full of thrilling races, new friends, and the realisation that his dream of becoming a Formula 1 driver was getting closer. He was proving to himself and others that he belonged in the big leagues. With each race, his confidence grew, his skills sharpened, and his passion for racing burned brighter than ever.

The Winning Formula

Zooming around the track in Formula 4 is like living inside a high-speed video game, and Pierre was right in the action! But racing wasn't just about going fast; it was also about using skills and strategy to outsmart the competition.

Imagine a super-charged game of tag where instead of running, you're driving incredibly fast cars around a winding track. You need to be quick, agile, and always think ahead. That's where skill and strategy come into play!

Speed is crucial. Pierre had to push his car to its limits, making sure to extract every bit of power from the engine. He needed to master taking corners at high speeds, accelerating smoothly, and finding the perfect racing line to gain an edge. It was like a high-speed dance, where each movement had to be precise and perfectly timed.

But speed alone wasn't enough. Pierre also needed skill. He had to control his car even when it slid or bounced over bumps. He needed to know when to brake, when to speed up, and when to take risks. It was like being a superhero, using quick reflexes and instincts to navigate the track with incredible precision.

Then there was strategy. Racing wasn't just about being fast; it was also about outsmarting your rivals. Pierre had to learn how to read the race, anticipate his competitors' moves, and make split-second decisions that could change the outcome. It was like playing chess at 200 miles per hour!

Pierre spent hours studying tracks, learning every curve, bump, and overtaking spot. He analysed his own performance and watched videos of other drivers to pick up tips and tricks.

But the most crucial part of Pierre's strategy was his mindset. Racing was as much a mental game as a physical one. He had to stay calm under pressure, focus on his goals, and never give up, even when things got tough. Believing in himself and his abilities was key.

With each race, Pierre's speed, skill, and strategy improved. He became a formidable driver on the track, able to outpace and outthink his rivals. He was proving he had the winning formula that could take him all the way to the top.

So, the next time you face a challenge, remember Pierre's story. Success isn't just about being the fastest or the strongest; it's about using your skills, intelligence, and determination. And most importantly, it's about never giving up, even when the odds seem against you. With the right mindset and a lot of effort, you can achieve incredible things!

Pierre's Star Begins To Shine

Have you ever seen a shooting star zoom across the night sky? It's fast, bright, and leaves a trail of wonder. That's exactly how Pierre Gasly was starting to make a name for himself in Formula 4. He was becoming a rising star, capturing the attention of fans, teams, and even the media!

It wasn't just about winning races; it was about how Pierre raced. He was fearless, always pushing the limits and taking calculated risks. He was also incredibly consistent, rarely making mistakes and finishing near the top of the pack. He was like a superhero on wheels, amazing the crowd with his daring moves and quick reflexes.

People started talking about Pierre, not just in the racing world but also in his hometown and beyond. He was becoming a local hero, inspiring kids who dreamed of racing like him. His name appeared in newspapers and magazines, and he was even starting to get recognized on the street!

Imagine you're playing a video game and you're scoring high points and unlocking achievements. Everyone starts noticing how great you are, and they cheer you on. That's the buzz Pierre was creating in the racing world.

But it wasn't just about fame. Pierre's success was catching the eye of professional racing teams. They saw his talent, dedication, and potential to be a champion. They knew he was a special driver with the potential to reach the top.

It was like being scouted for your favourite sports team! Imagine getting a call from a professional coach inviting you to join their team. That's the kind of opportunity Pierre was starting to get.

With success came even more pressure. Expectations were higher, the competition tougher, and the stakes greater. But Pierre was ready for it. He knew this was his chance to shine and prove he belonged in the professional racing world.

And shine he did! Pierre continued to win races, impress crowds, and catch the eye of racing insiders. He was making a name for himself not just as a fast driver but as a true champion in the making. His passion, dedication, and belief in himself were paying off, and the world was starting to take notice.

Pierre's story shows that with hard work, talent, and a bit of luck, you can achieve amazing things. It's about chasing your dreams, even when they seem far away, and never giving up, even when the path gets tough. So, the next time you're working towards a goal, remember Pierre's example. Keep pushing, keep striving, and who knows you might become the next rising star in your own field!

5.

THE ROLLERCOASTER RIDE

The Highs of Winning : Zoom Zoom To The Top!

Imagine standing on the highest podium you've ever seen, holding a shiny trophy and beaming with joy. Confetti falls like a colourful shower, and the crowd erupts in cheers and applause. It's your moment of triumph, your time to shine! That's exactly how Pierre felt every time he won a race in Formula 4. It was like a party on wheels, celebrating speed, skill, and pure excitement!

Every victory felt like an explosion of fireworks, filling Pierre's heart with happiness and thrill. As he crossed the finish line first, the checkered flag waved like a magical signal, and time seemed to slow down just for him. He'd take a deep breath, savouring the sweet taste of success, and then let out a triumphant "Yes!"

But the real celebration happened after the race. Pierre would get out of his car, his adrenaline still racing, and be greeted by his team. They'd hug, high-five, and dance around as if they'd just won a lottery! It was a team effort, and everyone deserved to enjoy the victory.

Next came the podium ceremony, where Pierre would stand proudly, holding his trophy high. He'd wave to the cheering crowd, his smile stretching from ear to ear. It was a magical moment, a testament to all the hard work and dedication that brought him here.

And then, of course, there was the champagne shower! A racing tradition that's all about bubbly joy and celebration. Pierre would laugh and drench his teammates in fizzy fun. It was a reminder that while racing is serious, it's also about enjoying the moment and having a blast.

But winning wasn't just about the excitement and fun. It was also about the feeling of accomplishment, knowing that all those hours of practice, early mornings, and late nights had paid off. It was proof to himself that he was capable of great things, that his dreams were becoming reality.

Each win fired up Pierre's passion for racing, making him even more eager for success. It was like a delicious treat, leaving him craving more. He knew that even bigger challenges were ahead and tougher races to conquer, but he was ready. He was a champion in the making, and this was just the beginning!

So, whenever you achieve something amazing, whether it's winning a race, acing a test, or mastering a new skill, take a moment to celebrate your success. Feel the rush of excitement, the pride in your achievement, and the joy of sharing it with those you care about. And most importantly, let that victory inspire you to keep dreaming big, working hard, and never giving up. Like Pierre, you have the power to turn your dreams into reality!

Facing Setbacks and Disappointments

Imagine you're building a gigantic LEGO castle. After days of careful construction, it's looking fantastic! But then, **crash!** Your little brother accidentally knocks it over, and everything falls apart. Frustrating, right? That's kind of how Pierre felt during his racing career. Not every race was a win, and there were certainly some bumps along the way.

Even the best racers face tough days. Sometimes the car doesn't perform well, tires lose grip, or another driver's mistake impacts everyone. Occasionally, it's simply not your day, and you end up further back than you hoped. It's like losing all your lives in a video game disappointing and tough to recover from.

Pierre faced his share of setbacks and disappointments. There were races where he crashed, made mistakes, or just couldn't keep up with the competition. It was frustrating and made him question himself at times. He wondered if he was good enough to be a champion.

But Pierre didn't let these setbacks define him. He understood that even top athletes encounter challenges. It's part of the journey and makes achieving your dreams all the more rewarding.

Think of it like learning to ride a bike. You might fall a few times and scrape your knee, but that doesn't mean you should give up. It just means you need to get back up, brush yourself off, and try again. That's exactly what Pierre did.

Whenever Pierre encountered a setback, he would take a deep breath, figure out what went wrong, and find ways to improve. He'd consult with his team, review race data, and practise harder. Each setback was a chance to learn, grow, and come back stronger.

It wasn't always easy. Pierre had moments of discouragement and wanted to give up. But he always remembered why he started racing: his love for cars, passion for competition, and dream of becoming a Formula 1 champion.

Pierre's resilience and determination in facing setbacks are truly inspiring. He demonstrates that making mistakes and having bad days are part of the process. What matters is how you respond. Do you give up, or do you use the challenges to fuel your determination?

So, the next time you face a setback, remember Pierre's story. Don't let it get you down. Instead, use it as a chance to learn, grow, and come back stronger. Even the greatest champions face challenges along their journey, and overcoming them makes achieving your dreams incredibly rewarding.

Turning Mistakes Into Turbo Boosts!

Ever tried baking cookies and accidentally added salt instead of sugar? Yuck! But even the best bakers make mistakes sometimes. The key is to learn from them and try again. That's exactly what Pierre did whenever he faced a setback in his racing career. He turned those mistakes into turbo boosts, propelling him forward even faster!

Imagine you're playing a video game and keep losing at a certain level. It's frustrating, right? But instead of giving up, you watch replays, study the level design, and figure out what went wrong. Then, you try again with new knowledge and determination. That's how Pierre approached his racing setbacks. He was like a detective, analysing every detail to uncover clues that would help him improve.

After a disappointing race, Pierre wouldn't just sulk. He'd review the race with his team, watch replays, and discuss what went wrong. He'd ask questions, listen to feedback, and figure out where he could improve. It was like solving a puzzle, and Pierre was determined to find the solution.

Sometimes the mistakes were obvious, like missing a breaking point or taking a turn too wide. Other times, they were more subtle, like a slight miscalculation in tire pressure or a minor error in strategy. No matter how big or small, Pierre was committed to learning from each mistake.

He'd spend hours analysing race data, examining every lap, turn, and decision. He compared his performance to other drivers, seeking ways to improve. He even practised on simulators, experimenting with different techniques and strategies.

But learning from mistakes wasn't just about data; it was also about the right mindset. Pierre understood that setbacks were a natural part of learning. He didn't let them discourage him; instead, he used them as motivation to work harder. He was like a bouncy ball, always rebounding higher and stronger after each fall.

And that's exactly what he did. After every setback, Pierre returned to the next race with renewed focus and determination. He applied what he'd learned, made adjustments to his driving, and pushed himself to be even better. It was like levelling up in a video game, gaining new skills and experience with each challenge.

Pierre's ability to learn from mistakes and bounce back stronger highlights his resilience and passion for racing. It shows us that setbacks are not failures but opportunities to learn and grow.

So, the next time you make a mistake, don't be too hard on yourself. Instead, take a deep breath, analyse what went wrong, and figure out how to do better next time. Remember, even the greatest champions face setbacks. It's all part of the journey, and overcoming these challenges makes achieving your dreams all the more rewarding.

6.

THE FRENCH FLYER

Zooming For The Tricolore!

Imagine being selected to represent your country in a major international event in your favourite sport. You'd be overflowing with pride, wouldn't you? That's precisely how Pierre felt when he began racing in global championships. He was no longer racing just for himself; he was representing France on the world stage!

It was an immense honour for Pierre, and he took the responsibility very seriously. He understood that he was carrying the hopes and dreams of countless French racing fans. Every time he got into his car, he wore the colours of his country—the iconic blue, white, and red of the French flag. It was like being a superhero, defending his nation's pride!

Competing internationally brought a whole new level of excitement. Pierre travelled to various countries, explored new cultures, and raced against top young drivers from around the world. It was an adventurous journey, filled with thrilling races, exotic locations, and the opportunity to make friends from all corners of the globe.

But it wasn't just about the travel and excitement. Pierre knew he was also a representative of France, a role model for those aspiring to achieve greatness. He aimed to demonstrate that French drivers were skilled, determined, and capable of standing toe-to-toe with the best.

Whenever Pierre stood on the podium and the French national anthem played, with the flag waving beside him, it was a moment of immense national pride.

He was proving to the world that France was a formidable force in motorsport.

Pierre's success on the international circuit inspired countless young people in France. They saw him as a hero who had risen from a small town to achieve his dreams through hard work and dedication. He became a symbol of hope, showing that anything is possible with belief and perseverance.

Pierre's journey from a young car enthusiast to a proud national representative is truly inspiring. It illustrates that dreams can lead to incredible places, that hard work can yield great results, and that you can make your family, community, and country proud.

So, when you pursue your passions, remember Pierre's story. Whether it's in sports, music, art, or another field, you have the power to inspire others and make a significant impact. Who knows? You might one day be representing your country on the global stage, just like Pierre Gasly!

France's Racing Hero

Picture your favourite sports team winning a championship, and the entire city erupts in celebration! People are waving flags, honking horns, and revelling in the moment. That's the kind of excitement Pierre Gasly stirred in France as he advanced in motorsport. He wasn't just a racer; he was becoming a national hero, a source of pride for the entire nation!

Every time Pierre won a race, it felt like a victory for all of France. People gathered around their TVs, cheering him on and holding their breath as he sped around the track. When he crossed the finish line first, the whole country celebrated as if there was a nationwide party from the Eiffel Tower to the French Riviera!

Newspapers and magazines would feature Pierre on their covers, hailing him as a rising star and future champion. Children hung posters of him in their rooms, dreaming of one day following in his footsteps. He became an inspiration for a generation of young French racing fans.

Pierre's achievements went beyond just winning races. He represented France with honour and dignity, always humble in victory, gracious in defeat, and a true ambassador for his country. He showed the world that French drivers were not only talented but also respectful and sportsmanlike.

Imagine being at school and winning a major competition. Your teachers, classmates, and parents are all immensely proud of you. That's how the whole of France felt about Pierre. He was their champion and hometown hero, and they couldn't be prouder.

Pierre's accomplishments resonated deeply with the French people, symbolising that big dreams can come true even from a small country. He proved that with hard work, dedication, and a bit of French flair, you can achieve anything.

What's truly inspiring about Pierre's story is how he embraced his role as a national hero. He recognized the impact he had on young people and took that responsibility seriously. He visited schools, gave talks, and even started a foundation to support aspiring young racers.

Pierre's story is a reminder that we can all make a difference, regardless of where we come from or what our dreams are. It's about using our talents and passions to inspire others, contribute to our communities, and make our countries proud.

So, when you achieve something special, remember Pierre's example. Celebrate your success, share your joy, and use your platform to create a positive impact. Like Pierre, you have the potential to be a hero not just on the racetrack, but in the hearts and minds of people everywhere!

Inspiring Young Racers: Pierre's Pit Crew Of Dreams

Imagine having a superhero as your role model, someone who not only accomplishes incredible feats but also encourages you to reach for the stars. That's what Pierre Gasly became for countless young racing fans around the world, especially in France. He was like a supercharged battery, energising dreams and sparking passions in the hearts of aspiring racers everywhere!

Kids watched Pierre's races with wide-eyed amazement, their hearts racing with excitement. They saw him bravely overtake rivals, expertly handle tricky corners, and celebrate his wins with infectious enthusiasm. Pierre showed them that dreams could indeed come true, proving that a kid from a small town could rise to the top of the racing world.

Pierre's story resonated with young people because it was relatable. He wasn't born into a racing dynasty or handed an easy path to success. Instead, he worked hard, faced numerous challenges, and never gave up on his dreams. He became a living testament to the power of passion, persistence, and self-belief.

Think of it like playing a video game where you see someone exceptionally skilled. At first, it seems impossible to reach their level. But then you learn that they started just like you, practising diligently, learning from their errors, and persisting. Their success suddenly seems attainable. That's the inspiration Pierre provided to young racers.

Pierre didn't just inspire through his racing; he actively engaged with his fans. He visited schools to share his journey, answered questions, signed autographs, and even allowed kids to sit in his race car. It was like meeting a superhero in person!

He also started a foundation to help young aspiring racers, providing them with the resources and opportunities to train, compete, and pursue their dreams. Pierre wanted to give back to the sport that had given him so much and help the next generation of racers realise their full potential.

Pierre's influence reached far beyond France. Young racers from around the globe looked up to him, inspired by his achievements and his story. He became a role model for anyone who dared to dream big, reminding them that with hard work, dedication, and a bit of speed, anything is possible.

So, when you feel discouraged or doubt your abilities, remember Pierre Gasly. Remember the kid who loved cars, chased his dreams relentlessly, and became a hero to millions. Let his story inspire you to keep pushing forward, to never give up on your passions, and to always believe in yourself. Just like Pierre, you have the power to achieve great things and make a positive impact on the world!

7.

NEVER GIVE UP

Pierre's "Never Give Up" Spirit

Imagine you're zooming down a go-kart track, feeling the wind rush by, when suddenly, BAM! You hit a bump and spin out of control. It's a bit nerve-wracking, isn't it? But what do you do next? Do you throw in the towel, or do you get back in the kart and continue racing? Pierre Gasly always chose to keep going. He faced adversity head-on, much like a knight charging bravely into battle!

Life, much like racing, is filled with unforeseen obstacles and challenges. There will be bumps, detours, and even flat tires. What distinguishes champions is their ability to overcome these difficulties, to pick themselves up, and to keep pushing forward. Pierre's path to Formula 1 was no different. He encountered numerous hurdles, but he never let them stop him.

One significant challenge Pierre faced was the loss of his close friend and fellow racer, Anthoine Hubert. This tragic event deeply affected Pierre, leading him to question whether racing was worth the risk and whether he could continue pursuing his dreams in such sorrowful circumstances.

However, Pierre didn't allow grief to overwhelm him. He channelled his sorrow into determination, dedicating his efforts to honouring Anthoine's memory by racing with even greater intensity. Despite the tough times, Pierre demonstrated incredible strength and resilience, showing that even in the darkest moments, hope remains.

Another challenge Pierre encountered was the immense pressure to perform. As he progressed through motorsport, the expectations grew higher and higher. Every race was scrutinised, and every mistake was highlighted. It felt like being under a massive spotlight, with everyone watching his every move.

Yet, Pierre didn't let the pressure deter him. He used it as motivation, a sign that he was on the right track and that people believed in his abilities. He learned to manage stress, stay focused, and remain committed to his goals.

Pierre also faced setbacks on the track, including accidents, mechanical issues, and races where he didn't perform at his best. These moments were frustrating and could easily lead to discouragement. But Pierre always rebounded.

He would review his mistakes, learn from them, and come back stronger. Each setback was like a level-up in a video game, gaining experience from each challenge he overcame. He understood that setbacks were just temporary obstacles on his path to success.

Pierre's ability to confront adversity is a testament to his character and unwavering spirit. He demonstrates that feeling sad, frustrated, or scared when faced with challenges is normal. What truly matters is how we respond. Do we let these challenges defeat us, or do we use them as motivation to become stronger?

So, when you face a challenge, remember Pierre's story. Don't shy away from your fears or obstacles. Keep moving forward, even when the road is rough. With courage, determination, and a never-give-up attitude, you can achieve your goals. Just like Pierre Gasly, you can turn adversity into an opportunity to excel!

The Secret Ingredient: Hard Work And Dedication

Imagine you're baking a cake. You have all the necessary ingredients: flour, sugar, eggs, and chocolate chips. But if you don't mix them together, bake them, and be patient, you won't end up with a delicious cake! Achieving your dreams is similar. You need talent, passion, and a bit of luck. But the most crucial ingredient is hard work and dedication. Pierre Gasly understands this better than anyone!

From a young age, Pierre knew that becoming a Formula 1 driver wouldn't be straightforward. It wasn't just about having a passion for cars or natural talent; it required putting in the hours, effort, and commitment. It meant showing up every day, even when you're exhausted or discouraged, and giving it your best.

Think of it like building a LEGO masterpiece. You can't just snap the pieces together and expect perfection. You need to follow instructions, be patient, and sometimes start over if things don't go as planned. That's how Pierre approached his racing career. He recognized that each practice session, each training drill, and each race was an opportunity to improve, learn, and get closer to his goal.

Pierre's commitment was remarkable. He dedicated countless hours to physical training, enhancing his strength and endurance. He analysed race data, studied his competitors, and refined his driving techniques. He even practised on simulators, improving his skills and familiarising himself with various tracks.

It wasn't always enjoyable. There were early mornings, late nights, and missed social events. Sometimes Pierre felt exhausted or frustrated, but he never quit. He understood that every sacrifice was an investment in his future, a step towards his dream.

Pierre's dedication went beyond physical training. It also involved mental focus and resilience. Racing is a high-pressure sport where quick decisions are crucial. Pierre had to learn to remain calm under pressure, block out distractions, and stay focused even when things didn't go as planned.

It was like training to be a superhero, pushing both mind and body to their limits. He was constantly challenging himself, learning from mistakes, and striving for excellence.

Pierre's journey highlights that there are no shortcuts to success. It requires hard work, dedication, and a willingness to go the extra mile. But the rewards are immense. When you're passionate and willing to put in the effort, amazing things can happen.

So, when you're working towards a goal, remember Pierre's example. Don't shy away from hard work, sacrifices, and maintaining focus, even when things get tough. With dedication and perseverance, you can achieve anything. Just like Pierre Gasly, you can turn your dreams into reality!

Turning Dreams into Reality: From Toy Cars to the Real Deal!

Imagine building a sandcastle on the beach. You start with a small pile of sand, but with each scoop and pat, it grows larger and more impressive. You add towers, moats, and tiny flags. Before long, you've created an extraordinary castle, something you once only imagined. This is similar to how Pierre Gasly turned his dreams into reality. He began with a small passion, and through each step, race, and victory, he built an exceptional career in Formula 1 racing!

It all started with toy cars, racing around his room, fueled by his imagination and love for speed. But Pierre didn't just dream; he took action. He started go-karting, learning the basics, and refining his skills. He faced numerous challenges, setbacks, and fierce competition, but he never gave up. He was like a determined builder, adding piece by piece to his dream, never losing sight of the final masterpiece.

As Pierre advanced in motorsport, his dreams expanded. He set his sights on Formula 1, the ultimate racing stage where only the top competitors are seen. It was a daunting goal, but Pierre was undaunted. He believed that with hard work, dedication, and a touch of luck, he could achieve it.

And one day, it happened. Pierre Gasly, the boy who adored cars, made his debut in Formula 1. It was a surreal achievement, the result of years of dreaming, striving, and perseverance. He was finally living his dream, racing alongside his idols on the world's most prestigious tracks.

The journey wasn't easy. Formula 1 is a high-stakes world with immense pressure and fierce competition. But Pierre met the challenge head-on, proving his worth with each race. Despite facing obstacles, setbacks, and heartbreak, he never lost his passion or determination.

Then came the ultimate reward: Pierre's first Formula 1 victory. It was a moment of pure joy, reflecting his incredible talent and relentless spirit. He had transformed his childhood dream into reality, demonstrating that with self-belief and perseverance, anything is possible.

Pierre's story is a powerful reminder that dreams are not just fleeting ideas; they are blueprints for the future, waiting to be realised. It teaches us that with passion, persistence, and hard work, we can make our dreams come true, no matter how ambitious they may seem.

So, the next time you dream of something extraordinary, remember Pierre Gasly. Remember the boy who loved cars, who dared to dream big, and who turned his passion into a profession. Let his story inspire you to chase your own dreams, build your own castles, and never give up on what you believe in. With the right mindset and determination, you can achieve anything. The world is your racetrack, and it's time to start your engines!!

8.

LIFE IN THE FAST LANE

The Fast And The Furious... Off The Track!

Ever wondered what life is like for a Formula 1 driver when they're not racing at incredible speeds? It's not just about the excitement and fame! Pierre Gasly's life is a whirlwind of training, travel, and teamwork. Let's take a behind-the-scenes look at what it takes to make those race day victories happen!

Think of it like a superhero movie. You see the hero saving the day and fighting villains, but there's a whole team working behind the scenes – the costume designers, stunt coordinators, and special effects experts. In Formula 1, Pierre might be the one driving the car, but he has a whole team helping him succeed.

First up, there's the intense training. Pierre trains like an athlete, pushing his body to stay in top shape. He spends hours in the gym, lifting weights, doing cardio, and working on his reflexes. He even has special exercises to strengthen his neck muscles because the G-forces during a race can be enormous! It's like being a superhero in training, getting ready for the ultimate challenge.

Then there's the travel. Pierre travels all around the world, racing in different countries almost every other week. He's like an adventurous explorer, discovering new places and cultures. But it's not just about sightseeing. He has to adjust to different time zones, climates, and track conditions. It's like a real-life video game, with each new location presenting its own set of challenges.

And then there's teamwork. Pierre's team is like a pit crew, working hard to make sure his car is perfect for every race. They're the engineers, mechanics, strategists, and support staff who keep everything running smoothly. It's like a well-oiled machine, where everyone plays a crucial role in Pierre's success.

But behind all the serious work, Pierre and his team also know how to have fun. They play pranks on each other, celebrate birthdays, and enjoy meals together. They're like a family, supporting each other through thick and thin.

Pierre's life behind the scenes shows the dedication and hard work required to be a Formula 1 driver. It's not just about talent; it's about countless hours of training, travelling, and having a supportive team.

So next time you watch a Formula 1 race, remember all the action happening behind the scenes. Think of Pierre and his team, working tirelessly to make those thrilling moments on the track possible. It's a reminder that success often involves a whole team working together, and that's truly inspiring!

The Glamour And Excitement Of Race Day

Imagine the most exciting, colourful party you've ever been to, but instead of dancing, everyone is cheering for super-fast cars zooming around a track! That's what race day in Formula 1 is like, and it's the moment Pierre Gasly lives for!

Race day is packed with glitz, glamour, and heart-pounding excitement. The atmosphere is electric, the energy is contagious, and the anticipation is almost too much to handle. It's like the grand finale of a superhero movie, where everything builds up to one epic showdown!

Pierre starts his day early, feeling a mix of nerves and excitement. He eats a healthy breakfast, stretches his muscles, and goes through his mental checklist, preparing for the challenges ahead. It's like a hero getting ready for battle, sharpening his sword and polishing his armour!

Then it's off to the track, where the real action begins. Pierre walks through the paddock, surrounded by fans, cameras, and the buzz of race day preparations. It's like walking down a red carpet, with everyone cheering and wanting to see the star of the show.

He puts on his fireproof suit, helmet, and gloves, transforming into a racing superhero. He climbs into his car, the engine roaring to life, and feels a rush of adrenaline. It's time to race!

The starting grid is a symphony of sights and sounds. The cars lined up, their engines revving, the crowd cheering, and the tension building with each passing second. It's like the countdown to a rocket launch, with everyone holding their breath, waiting for liftoff.

Then, the lights go out, and it's GO! Pierre accelerates, his car shooting forward like a bullet. The crowd roars, colours blur, and the world becomes a whirlwind of speed and sound. It's an experience like no other, a pure rush of adrenaline that few people ever get to feel.

Throughout the race, Pierre stays laser-focused. He's making split-second decisions, reacting to his opponents, and pushing his car to the limit. It's like playing a video game on the hardest level, where every move matters and every mistake can be costly.

But race day is also about the fans. Thousands of people come from all over the world to witness the spectacle, cheer for their favourite drivers, and soak in the excitement. They wave flags, wear team colours, and create an atmosphere that's unforgettable.

For Pierre, the fans make race day extra special. Their energy fuels his passion, their cheers lift his spirits, and their support motivates him to push even harder. It's a connection that goes beyond the track, a shared love for the sport that unites people from all walks of life.

So next time you watch a Formula 1 race, remember the glamour and excitement of race day. Think of Pierre Gasly, the boy who loved cars, living his dream and inspiring millions around the world. It's a reminder that with passion, dedication, and a bit of speed, you can achieve anything. And who knows? Maybe one day you'll be the one standing on the podium, celebrating your own hard-earned victory!

Balancing Act: Racing, Friends, And... Laundry?!

Imagine juggling flaming torches while riding a unicycle on a tightrope! That's kind of what it's like for Pierre Gasly to balance his thrilling Formula 1 career with his personal life. It's a tricky act, but Pierre's got it down to an art!

Being a Formula 1 driver is like being a rock star, but instead of strumming a guitar, you're zooming around racetracks at lightning speeds. It's glamorous, thrilling, and takes up a *lot* of time! Pierre spends most of his days training, travelling, and working with his team. It's a full-time job, plus a bit more!

But Pierre isn't just a racing machine. He's also a regular person who enjoys hanging out with friends, playing video games, and even doing his own laundry (yes, even superheroes have chores!). Finding time for all of this can be tricky, but Pierre has some clever strategies.

Think of it like managing a super-busy schedule packed with school, homework, sports practice, and maybe even a part-time job. It's a lot to handle, but with good organisation and time management, you can make it work. That's exactly what Pierre does.

He's like a master planner, carefully organising his days to fit everything in. He might start with a morning workout, followed by a meeting with his engineers, then a quick lunch with family, and finish with simulator practice in the afternoon. It's a jam-packed schedule, but Pierre makes it look easy.

Of course, sometimes things get chaotic. Unexpected delays, last-minute changes, and even jet lag can disrupt even the best plans. But

Pierre has learned to be flexible and adaptable. He's like a ninja, always ready to change course and tackle any challenge that comes his way.

Even though his racing career takes up a lot of his time, Pierre never forgets the importance of his personal life. He makes sure to carve out time for friends and family, whether it's a quick video call, a weekend trip, or just a cosy movie night at home. He knows that having a strong support system is crucial for his happiness and well-being.

Pierre's ability to balance his demanding career with his personal life is truly inspiring. It shows us that even when we're chasing our dreams, it's important to make time for the people and things we love. It's about finding that perfect balance, where we can pursue our passions while still enjoying a fulfilling life.

So next time you're feeling overwhelmed by a busy schedule, remember Pierre's example. Take a deep breath, prioritise what's important, and don't be afraid to ask for help. And most importantly, remember to have fun along the way!

Just like Pierre, you can achieve great things while still enjoying the journey.

9.

INSPIRING THE NEXT GENERATION

Follow Your Passion And Chase Your Dreams

Imagine if you had a superpower. Maybe it's singing, drawing, dancing, or even building robots. It's something that makes your heart race and your eyes light up every time you do it. That special thing is your passion! It's what makes you amazing and unique. For Pierre Gasly, his superpower was his love for cars and racing, and he chased that passion all the way to becoming a Formula 1 driver.

From the time he was very young, Pierre knew that cars were his *thing*. He was fascinated by everything about them – the speed, the sound, the way they looked, and even the smell of burning tires! He would spend hours playing with his toy cars, pretending to race them, and watching car races on TV. He didn't just like cars; they filled him with excitement, joy, and energy. He dreamed of the day when he could become a race car driver himself.

But following your passion isn't always easy. Sometimes people may tell you that your dreams are too big or too hard to achieve. They might say it's impossible. But Pierre didn't listen to those voices. He followed his heart and decided to pursue his dreams, even when things got challenging or when people tried to steer him toward a different, safer path.

Think of your dream like a treasure hunt. You have a map, and the treasure chest is hidden somewhere amazing. The journey to find it is full of twists, turns, and obstacles. Some people might tell you to give up because it's too hard, but deep down, you know that treasure is out there waiting for you. That's how Pierre felt about becoming a Formula 1 driver. He knew it wouldn't be easy, but he was determined to chase his dream and keep going, no matter what.

Pierre's journey wasn't smooth all the time. There were challenges, setbacks, and moments when he doubted himself. But his love for racing kept him going, like a guiding star that helped him stay on course. Every time he felt like giving up, he thought about how much he loved being on the racetrack. That passion gave him strength and pushed him forward.

Pierre worked hard, trained every day, and surrounded himself with people who believed in him. They encouraged him to keep going and reminded him of how far he had come. Through all of his hard work, he never lost sight of what he loved about racing: the thrill, the excitement, and the feeling of crossing the finish line.

Then, one day, his dream came true. Pierre Gasly, the kid who loved cars, became a Formula 1 driver! He stood on the podium, the checkered flag waving, and the crowd cheering his name. His journey wasn't easy, but he proved that with passion, hard work, and belief in yourself, you can achieve the impossible.

Pierre's story shows all of us that following your passion is worth it. No matter how big or small your dream is, it's always worth chasing. And even if the road is hard, don't let go of what makes you happy. With dedication, effort, and a little courage, you can turn your dreams into something amazing.

Believe In Yourself And Never Give Up!

Picture yourself trying to learn a new skateboard trick. You fall and scrape your knee. It's frustrating, and you might feel like giving up. But then you remember Pierre Gasly, the Formula 1 champion who never gave up on his dreams. Even when the road was tough, he believed in himself and kept pushing forward. So, you dust yourself off, get back on your board, and keep trying until you finally land that trick. That's the power of never giving up!

Pierre's road to becoming a Formula 1 driver was full of challenges. He faced tough competition, had mechanical failures, and experienced moments when he wasn't sure if he could succeed. But even during the toughest times, Pierre believed in himself. He knew he had the talent and determination to achieve his dreams.

Imagine climbing a mountain. The journey is long and difficult, and there are moments when you want to turn back. But if you keep taking one step at a time and believe you can reach the top, you will eventually get there. That's exactly how Pierre felt as he pursued his dreams. He never lost sight of his goal, even when the climb got steep.

Pierre's belief in himself was like a shield that protected him from doubt and negativity. He surrounded himself with people who supported him and reminded him of his strengths. No one could convince him that his dreams were impossible because Pierre knew his passion would take him far.

But self-belief wasn't the only thing that helped Pierre succeed. He was also *resilient*. That means he learned how to bounce back from every challenge.

Every time something went wrong, Pierre would dust himself off, analyse what happened, and try again. He kept getting better and better, using every mistake as a chance to grow.

Pierre's journey reminds us that believing in yourself and staying resilient are the keys to achieving success. Even when things are tough, you have the power to overcome challenges, learn from them, and keep moving forward.

Hard Work: Pedal To The Metal!

Imagine building the coolest sandcastle ever. You've got your bucket and shovel, but this is going to take more than a few scoops of sand. You'll need to work hard, carefully shaping every tower and wall. It might take hours or even days! But with each bit of effort, your masterpiece grows. That's exactly what Pierre Gasly's journey was like as he worked his way to becoming a Formula 1 driver.

Pierre knew that to reach his dream, it wasn't just about being talented, he had to put in the effort every single day. He practised on the racetrack, studied other drivers, worked out to stay strong, and constantly improved his skills. He woke up early, stayed up late, and dedicated himself to becoming the best driver he could be.

There were times when Pierre was tired or frustrated. But even on those tough days, he reminded himself that hard work was the only way to reach his goals. Every drop of sweat, every practice lap, every early morning was one step closer to the dream. Like building a giant sandcastle, each small effort added up to something incredible.

Hard work doesn't just mean physical effort. Pierre also had to train his mind. Racing is a high-pressure sport, and Pierre needed to stay calm and focused, even in the most intense moments. He taught himself to stay cool under pressure, to make quick decisions, and to keep pushing forward, no matter what.

Pierre's story is a reminder that nothing great comes without effort. To reach your dreams, you'll need to work hard, stay focused, and never give up. Even when the road is difficult, keep going. Because just like Pierre Gasly, you have the power to make your dreams come true!

So, what are you waiting for? Start chasing your passion, put in the work, believe in yourself, and never give up. The world is waiting for you to show it what you're made of!

CONCLUSION

And there you have it, my friends Pierre Gasly's thrilling journey has crossed the finish line! We've raced through his life, from a little boy who adored toy cars to a full-fledged Formula 1 champion. It's been an exciting adventure, packed with twists, turns, and heart-pounding "**zoom zoom**!" moments that kept us cheering for more.

We've seen Pierre's love for racing explode like a rocket, pushing him toward his biggest dreams. We stood by as he faced obstacles, bounced back from tough times, and refused to give up. His story is filled with incredible dedication, a strong spirit, and an endless excitement for doing what he loves most racing at lightning speeds!

But guess what? Pierre's journey isn't just about fast cars and winning races. It's a reminder to all of us that dreams **do** come true, as long as you're ready to put in the work, stay focused, and keep your eyes on the goal. It's about how passion, the love for something that makes you excited, can take you to amazing places. It also shows the importance of teamwork and how powerful believing in yourself can be.

The most important lesson we've learned from Pierre's story is that **anything** is possible, no matter how big or small your dream is. You just have to be brave enough to follow it. Maybe your passion is soccer, art, science, or even something totally unique whatever it is, embrace it, let it fill your heart with excitement, and let it guide you through life's journey. Even when things get tough, or you hit a few bumps in the road, keep going. Pierre's journey shows us that if you keep moving forward and try your best, you'll go far!

So, as we wrap up this amazing adventure, let's take Pierre's story as a challenge. Let's dream as big as we can, work as hard as we can, and never let anyone tell us we can't achieve something incredible. Find what makes you light up inside, chase it with all your energy, and use it to make the world a better and more exciting place.

Remember, life is like a long race, but it's also filled with awesome opportunities. So strap in, press the gas pedal, and let your dreams be your fuel! Just like Pierre Gasly, you have the power to make your dreams come true.

Now go out there, take the wheel, and show the world what you're made of!

GLOSSARY

Zoom Zoom! Your Go-To Guide To Racing Lingo

Ever felt like racing is a secret club with its own special language? No worries you're about to become a racing pro! Get ready to dive into this super-fun and easy-to-understand glossary of racing terms, designed to make you sound like an expert in no time. Let's go!

1. **Checkered Flag:** Imagine you're running a race, and at the end, there's a giant flag waving, saying "You did it!"

That's the checkered flag! It's black and white, and when it waves, it means the race is over and someone just crossed the finish line first time to celebrate!

2. Pit Stop: Picture this: you're on a long road trip and you pull over for a super-quick snack or a bathroom break. In racing, a pit stop is when the car pulls into the pit lane for things like a fast tire change, refueling, or quick repairs. The faster the team works, the quicker the car gets back in the race it's all about speed and teamwork!

3. Pole Position: Think of it like being first in line for the biggest, coolest roller coaster at the amusement park! In racing, pole position means starting the race at the very front, giving the driver the best chance to zoom ahead of everyone else.

4. Overtake: Ever been in a race with your friends and suddenly, one of you sprints ahead? That's an overtake! It's when a driver speeds past another car, and it's one of the most exciting parts of racing it can totally change who's going to win!

5. Podium: Imagine winning a school talent show and standing on the winner's stage, cheering with a huge smile! In racing, the podium is where the top three drivers stand after the race, celebrating their awesome achievement. Sometimes, they even spray champagne (or in your case, maybe sparkling juice)!

6. G-Force: Have you ever been on a rollercoaster and felt like you were being squished into your seat as it zoomed around the track? That's G-force! In racing, when drivers accelerate really fast, they feel this intense force pushing them back in their seat. It's like the ride of a lifetime, every single race!

7. Paddock: Imagine a backstage area at your favorite concert, but instead of musicians, it's packed with fast cars, drivers, and their crews getting ready to race! That's the paddock where all the behind-the-scenes action happens before and after the race.

8. Formation Lap: Think of this as a warm-up lap, like stretching before a big race at school. The cars slowly drive around the track, warming up their tires and engines, getting ready for the real action to start!

9. Grid: The grid is like the starting line of a big race, but instead of just running shoes, it's filled with roaring engines and high-speed cars! The drivers line up based on their qualifying positions, waiting for the signal to start the race.

10. DRS (Drag Reduction System): This is a bit like having a secret speed boost in a video game! DRS is a special system in Formula 1 cars that helps them go even faster on straight parts of the track by opening a flap on the rear wing. It's like hitting the "turbo" button!

Bonus Tip: Racing is full of cool abbreviations like F1 for Formula 1 or ERS for Energy Recovery System. Don't stress about remembering them all at once just enjoy learning as you go and have fun becoming a racing expert!

Now that you've got these awesome racing terms in your pocket, you're ready to impress your friends, family, and maybe even Pierre Gasly himself! Whether you're watching a race or imagining yourself behind the wheel, remember that with hard work, determination, and a love for what you do, you can accomplish anything. So, buckle up and get ready to race toward your dreams!

FUN FACTS ABOUT PIERRE

Here are some super cool and fun facts about Pierre Gasly that will make you feel like you're right there cheering him on at the racetrack. Ready to get inspired? Let's go in!

Zoom Zoom from a Young Age!
Picture this: most 6-year-olds are just learning how to tie their shoes, but Pierre? He was already racing go-karts! That's like being in kindergarten and knowing how to drive a mini race car! By starting so young, he got a head start on his dreams of becoming a Formula 1 superstar. If you have a big

dream, it's never too early to start chasing it!

A Football Fanatic

Before Pierre became the king of the racetrack, he had another dream becoming a soccer star! He's a huge fan of Paris Saint-Germain (PSG), one of the top soccer teams in France. Who knows, maybe some of those fancy soccer moves helped him develop quick reflexes on the racetrack! Just like Pierre, it's okay to have more than one passion sometimes one dream leads to another!

Lucky Number 10

Pierre's racing number, 10, isn't just a random choice; it's his lucky charm! He wore this number when he won a huge championship in 2013, and it also happens to be the number of his childhood hero, the legendary soccer player Zinedine Zidane. Talk about a number with double the magic! Whether it's a lucky number, a favorite pair of socks, or even a lucky charm, sometimes little things can bring us a lot of confidence.

Helmet Art

Pierre's racing helmets aren't just about safety they're works of art! He changes up his helmet designs for different races, depending on the weather or how he's feeling. It's kind of like picking out a cool new outfit for every big adventure. His helmets are one more way Pierre shows off his personality on the track. Just like him, you can express your unique style wherever you go!

Brains and Brawn

Did you know that Pierre is not only fast on the track but also a mastermind off it? He loves playing chess and tackling challenging puzzles. Racing isn't just about speed—it's about strategy too! Maybe his sharp thinking in chess helps him figure out the smartest moves during races. This shows that using both your body and your brain can lead to great things!

Fitness Tracker on His Finger

Here's something high-tech: Pierre wears a special ring that tracks his fitness levels, including his sleep, heart rate, and activity. It's like having a tiny coach wrapped around his finger, making sure he's always in peak condition for racing. Staying healthy is super important, and Pierre's always on top of his game with this nifty gadget!

Not Afraid to Speak Up

Pierre is known for being bold and honest. Whether it's on the racetrack or off, he's not afraid to share his thoughts, even if they're a bit controversial. He's got courage, not just behind the wheel but also when it comes to standing up for what he believes in. Speaking your mind can be just as powerful as racing to the finish line don't be afraid to use your voice!

A Love for Fashion

When he's not zipping around the track, Pierre has a flair for fashion! He's often spotted wearing trendy clothes and stylish sneakers. It wouldn't be surprising if one day he designs his own racing gear! Pierre shows that you can have different interests, and fashion is just another way he expresses his creative side. So, mix your hobbies and passions it's what makes you, **you**!

A Big Heart

Pierre doesn't just race to win he also gives back. He's involved in charity work and loves to help others in need. He's living proof that being a champion isn't just about winning trophies; it's about making the world a better place. Kindness is a superpower we all have, and Pierre uses his to make a positive impact, both on and off the track.

Multilingual Maestro

Being a globe-trotting race car driver means Pierre needs to communicate with people all over the world and he's a pro at it! He speaks French, English, and Italian, which definitely comes in handy when he's talking to his team and fans. Learning new languages can open up a whole world of possibilities!

So, there you have it Pierre Gasly is more than just a fast driver. He's a soccer-loving, fashion-forward, kind-hearted, multilingual racer who's passionate about what he does. His journey shows us that with hard work, dedication, and a little bit of flair, you can achieve anything you set your mind to. Whether you're chasing your own dreams or discovering new passions, remember Pierre's story and keep zooming toward your goals!

Trivia

1. What was Pierre's first love when it came to sports?

   (a) Tennis

   (b) Swimming

   (c) Soccer

   (d) Basketball

2. What is Pierre's lucky racing number?

   (a) 7

   (b) 10

   (c) 22

   (d) 44

3. Besides driving fast cars, what other skill is Pierre really good at?

(a) Playing the piano
(b) Painting
(c) Playing chess
(d) Cooking

4. What special technology does Pierre wear on his finger to help him stay fit?
(a) A smartwatch
(b) A fitness tracking ring
(c) A heart rate monitor armband
(d) A GPS tracker

5. What does Pierre love to do when he's not racing?
(a) Reading books
(b) Playing video games

(c) Expressing himself through fashion

(d) Hiking in the mountains

6. How many languages can Pierre speak?

(a) One

(b) Two

(c) Three

(d) Four

7. What sad event in 2019 deeply affected Pierre and the racing world?

(a) A major car accident

(b) The loss of a close friend and fellow racer

(c) A serious injury

(d) A team disqualification

8. What's the name of the special system on a Formula 1 car that helps it go even faster on straightaways?
    (a) KERS
    (b) DRS
    (c) ERS
    (d) GPS

9. Besides being a talented racer, what else is Pierre known for being?
    (a) Shy and reserved
    (b) Funny and goofy
    (c) Honest and outspoken
    (d) Quiet and introspective

Answers

1. (c)
2. (b)
3. (c)
4. (b)
5. (c)
6. (c)
7. (b)
8. (b)
9. (c)

Printed in Great Britain
by Amazon